Seasoned by the Seasons of Grace

Darlene D. Curl

Seasoned by the Seasons of Grace

ISBN: 978-1-7358359-6-9

Published by The Vision to Fruition Publishing House
www.vtfpublishing.com

Printed in the USA

Seasoned by the Seasons of Grace was presented to

____

on the _____ day of __________

in the year of ________ by

______________________________.

Dedication

T*his* book is dedicated to everyone I've crossed paths with in life thus far. Every encounter orchestrated and designed by God had a part in creating, molding, and shaping me into the woman I am (Sprinklings of all kinds of seasonings).

I am grateful for my Children, Grandchildren, all of my Maternal and Paternal Family members, Friends, Friends I consider Family, and my Inner Circle of Friends (there is a distinction between the levels of friendship).

I am thankful for All the Church Families I have been a part of growing up, during all my military tours, and upon settling in Maryland. I must include all the friends and co-workers I have grown to know and love over my 24 years of service that created my Military Family. As well as the people I have worked closely with since retirement that have impacted me in many ways in civilian life. For all you have given to me, I pray that you experience God like never before and that *"He will pour into your lap a good measure—pressed down, shaken together, and running over [with no space left for more]. For with the standard of measurement you use [when you do good to others], it will be measured to you in return."* Luke 6:38 (AMP)

Darlene D. Curl

"Living My Life Like It's Golden because I Love My Life…

Thank You, Lord, it's because of You."

Acknowledgments

I want to acknowledge my former Pastor, Anthony Johnson, who God saw fit to plant me within his ministry in November 2008 until the doors closed on July 31, 2017. Within this span of 9 years, I'd grown spiritually, mentally, and socially and formed some lifelong friendships with my brothers and sisters that I will always consider family because of the closeness our congregations came to be.

Having had the opportunity to serve in many roles within the ministry, the one that truly cultivated the most significant personal changes in me was alongside my Praise and Worship team. Throughout the years, I had the pleasure of serving with Lisa Harris, Lashanda Jones, Stella Murray, Felicia Brown, Lashanette Paris, D'Andrea Johnson, Jean Langston, Tanika Hart, Jasmine Mattocks, John Troutman, Kenny Muschette, Alvin Young, Roger Langston, Ronald Thornton, Warren Mattocks, Donald Jackson, Cameron Harris, Kevin Logan, and Jerry Nelson. If I have missed adding anyone's name that was a part of the Praise and Worship Team, please charge it to my head and not my heart.

This brings us to the Genesis of this book being written. There was a season when the Lord spoke to Anthony to move the Praise and Worship Team to a new level and create the Levitical Levites. We were challenged to create songs, sometimes collectively or individually, within the presence and influence of the Holy Spirit. Sometimes the words came first, and then the melody was worked out to match what was given. Other times, we'd have the musical melody and hear the words that should go with it, and we would create right there on the spot. It made for some indescribable preparation sessions that had us staying later than scheduled because the flow of the Spirit was such that you didn't want to leave His presence.

That which I didn't think I was able to do, was accomplished during this season, and I am thankful to Anthony for being obedient to God in what He instructed him to do with us. We were taken out of our comfort zone, encouraged to think outside the box, to flow in the Spirit, to quiet and still ourselves to hear God's voice, stretched in ways we haven't experienced, guided to do new things, molded and used by Him for the purposing. What was authored and ministered through us was for His Glory and the building of His

Kingdom by inspiring, consoling, and loving His children.

Thank you, Anthony, for facilitating the season of writing our songs at Light of Glory Ministries (affectionately known as LOGM) which made this book project possible. May God continue to bless you, D'andrea, and the family. Luke 6:38 says, *"Give, and it will be given to you. They will pour into your lap a good measure—pressed down, shaken together, and running over [with no space left for more]. For with the standard of measurement you use [when you do good to others], it will be measured to you in return."* (AMP)

I would also like to thank my family and close friends who are mentioned in the stories told that accompany the songs that were written. They have been my most present cheerleaders and contributors to what has taken place in my life: Veronica Robinson (Mother), Jelisa Curl & Tinisha Curl (Daughters), Justus (Granddaughter), Kersha (Sister-in-Law), Devon (Nephew), and Salomon (Nephew). My inner circle of friends birthed out of LOGM: Lisa H., Lashanda, Stella, Lashanette, Lawana Rose, LaKesha L. Williams, Lisa

McRae., and Felicia. Also, smiling down from heaven: Henry (Father), Dexter (Brother), and my beloved Grandmothers Katherine and Emma.

Darlene D. Curl

Table of Contents

Prayer

F*ather* God, Holy One, You are everything to me!

I thank you for this opportunity, in this season of my life, to share with others the words and messages conveyed within each song You have inspired in me to pen, record and share, along with my Light of Glory Ministries, New Light Vision Record Label brothers, and sisters.

My hope is that these messages will be received and resonate within each soul that will hear and listen. It is my hope these words will spark an interest in those who have yet to know You, and as a result, they'll have the desire to establish a relationship with You.

For those who already have that personal relationship with You but could use some encouragement in their day-to-day life experiences, may they find comfort in You, knowing they are not alone in what they're experiencing. I pray they reach a new level of intimacy with You.

Darlene D. Curl

In the mighty name, that is above all names, Jesus Christ, Our Lord and Savior, I pray.

Amen

Preface

O*riginally,* this project was supposed to be an album created under a ministry I was a part of called Light of Glory Ministries (LOGM) back in 2017. The title at first was called *Grounded,* in the sense that everything we go through is manageable when you are grounded and connected by your relationship with God and Christ. When the church dissolved and closed its doors for the last time on July 31, 2017, the project didn't go any further. All the songs were written and recorded and were in the stage of editing and being modified to finalize the album for release later that year.

After a year of my notes sitting around gathering dust, I kept having the feeling that I should still try to do something with this project because of how special it was, the potential of inspiring and encouraging others in what they go through in their day to day lives, along with all the hard work, time and effort put into it. The opportunity arrived to turn what was going to be a music album into a book with the help of my friend and Sister Lakesha L Williams (Author, Publisher, Entrepreneur).

With everything that has taken place in life, this project itself, and what this book speaks about, after much prayer, I was inspired to change the name to Seasoned by Seasons of Grace. As you read this book, it will give you some insight into my life experiences that have shaped and molded me into the woman I've become today.

The day when God created the perfect atmosphere and removed my three-year writer's block, allowing me to complete this book in 12 hours.

A Taste of What my Seasonings Produced

W*hat* I have come to learn so far in my life's journey is how God has always had me in the right place, at the right time, as a bridge to connect other people to each other in ministry, business, and the workplace. Sheryl, a friend I met during my last deployment in 2010/2011, helped me realize this as we talked one day at lunch before I rotated back home. I shared with her that I didn't know what my purpose in life was. We talked about my curiosity in reference to my purpose. As I recall, I knew how to do a little bit of a lot of things, and some would say I was a jack of all trades, mastering some.

I don't have a problem with tinkering around with things to see how they work, I can be a little OCDish, and when I needed to figure something out, I couldn't stop looking for ways to do it until I either exhausted all avenues or decided it just couldn't be accomplished or solved.

I also noticed how God would place me in positions to observe and hear things that would be helpful and assist others. Physically, my desk location at previous workplaces would be like the position of an eagle's nest, a vantage point to come into the knowledge of things over time, hearing conversations and statements made, to share smiles, greetings, and pleasantries.

I have experienced a lot of things, starting from my youth, that makes me wonder about the impact of the purpose God has created me for. I have been given the impression that His works through me and who I am, and what I am able to accomplish does matter, in such a way the weapons formed against me God would not let them prosper. My life matters in such a way that I actually contribute to and positively affect the atmosphere and environment around me, making a difference not only for my life in particular, but being a living testimony of God's Greatness, Love, Grace, and Mercy to those whose paths I come in contact with. Which causes a ripple effect of how they too can share in these experiences that would better their lives and show them God's perspective.

Seasoned by the Seasons of Grace

My existence was challenged many times, But God! First, I would say it started before I was a possibility when my father was told that he couldn't have children during his previous marriage, but when he and my mom met, the plan of God as written in Psalm 139:13-14, was set in motion.

"For You formed my innermost parts; You knit me [together] in my mother's womb. I will give thanks and praise to You, for I am fearfully and wonderfully made; Wonderful are Your works, and my soul knows it very well."

When my mom was eight months pregnant with me, she hit a deer as she was driving home from work (she was a Registered Nurse at the VA Hospital in Montrose, New York). When I was five months old, something caused my neck to swell, and doctors had to drain it; to this day, I still have the indentation of where the tube was inserted in my neck.

I was told that I had fallen down a flight of wooden stairs when I was 15 months old, where I lay motionless, and by the time my parents got to the bottom of the stairs, I started to move around and cry, without any injuries.

In the third grade, I was hit by a car while walking to Washington Street School, because I didn't listen to my mother when she said to only cross the street at the light, but I decided to run across between two parked cars. I remember the car being blue, and I think it was a TransAm. One of the ladies in the neighborhood sitting outside on her front porch saw what happened. I was temporarily knocked unconscious, and when I came to, I stood up when I realized what had happened (I think the fear and adrenaline of what my mom was going to do, replaced any pain that I might have felt.) The driver got out of his car and asked if I needed to be taken to the hospital, but I said I wasn't going to get into a stranger's car, and he said okay, got back into his car, and drove off. The lady sitting on her porch told me that I needed to go home and tell my mother, well, I wasn't about to do that, so I went back towards my house like I was going home, and instead went the long way around the block to cross the street at the light, out of the line of view of the lady. When I got to the school, I found out that some of my classmates had seen what happened too, because they were scared when I walked into the classroom and hearing them say, *"I thought you were dead when that car hit you."* But nope, my stubbornly Blessed self got up and went to school.

My parents didn't find out until months later when my best friend Sherrie's sister Shirl, told my mother. As you can imagine, life wasn't pleasant for me for a while. I had my first surgery at eight years old when I had to have my tonsils removed.

When I was around ten years old, I was in a car accident riding with my Grandmother Katherine, where my nose was fractured, and my knee was cut up. I still bear the scars. These are just some of the occurrences in the season of my youth that have contributed to creating the woman I am today, along with the following seasonings of accomplishments and tidbits of information I will share about myself.

- Daughter, Sister, Mother, Aunt, Ex-Wife, Airman, VoVo (Grandmother), Friend, Waitress, Business Owner, Contractor, Author, and Gardner

- Nick Names given to me by family – Squirt (my Dad called Squirt because I was a small baby) & Dee Dee (the rest of the family calls me Dee Dee)

Dad & Squirt

- Created my own Natural Skin Care Product Company/Business – Daily Desire LLC.
- Hosted my own Try & Buy Vendor event
- Registered with BMI as a Songwriter
- I have a Gospel Single Released - Lord You Are – September 22, 2015
- Sang Oh Happy Day on stage at Howard Theater Sunday Brunch
- I participated in a Tandem Sky Dive On my 44th Birthday

Seasoned by the Seasons of Grace

- Jumped off six waterfalls in the Dominican Republic
- I was picked by the ringmaster to dance the soul train line at Universal Soul Circus
- Bachelor's Degree in Psychology from American Military University
- Church Affiliations – AME Zion, COGIC, Baptist, Non-Denominational
- Was Vice President of a Non-Profit for 1 Year
- Visited many places overseas: Spain, France, Germany, Italy, Austria, Belgium, England, Japan, Korea, Jamaica, Costa Rica, Dominican Republic, Hawaii, Liechtenstein, Lithuania, Turkey, Cypress, Southwest Asia
- I love being outdoors, going on nature walks, hiking, exploring, Bowling, Rollercoasters, 5K events and wild rides
- I went on an Ice Slide & Sand Dune Rides in Southwest Asia
- Can cook, bake, grill, broil, fry, air fry, deep fry, sauté, and make drinks, which is a good reason to be a foodie.
- Animal Kingdom experiences: Rode a Horse in Spain and the Dominican Republic, Rode a

Camel in Southwest Asia, Pet and took a picture with a Boa Snake on the streets of NYC, along with a Cheetah and a hawk in Southwest Asia, and was surrounded by the pigeons of Venice Italy

I have a very adventurous spirit and love to try out new experiences.

Seasoned by the Seasons of Grace

Summer

J*ust* like in nature, during the seasons of Summer, everything in life is beautiful, in full bloom; there are great times experienced filled with vacations, warm weather, cookouts, and various trips. The song *Pleasant Things* was created out of many great memories connected with summer, which involves spending time with family and friends for as long as I remember starting as a child.

Being from Upstate New York in a city and town called Newburgh, there were many summers in my youth where I hung out with my cousins Yvette, Michelle, Tina, Detrice, Sonya, Yanicee, Curt, Tawana, Lorretta, Tina, Vernon, Robert, Catrell, my friends Lisa, Danielle, Crystal, Lawanda, and Sherrie, just to name a few. Then there were summers spent down south, in Cottageville, South Carolina, at my maternal grandmother's house with my cousins Deborah, Josephine, James, Marcus, Yolanda, Monica, Corrine, Chrissy, Craig, Faye, Toot, and Skeeter, which are the names I remember but there were others. Along with the children, whom I affectionately refer to as my down south friends, that lived up the road from my grandmother's house, Patricia and her brothers, Alice, Junie, and Moosey, again there were more, but I can't remember their names. I also experienced some of my Summers at the Robinson Family Reunions on my father's side of the family in Connecticut at Indian Wells State Park or the Lighthouse, playing with my cousins Darcey, Dana, Monica, Alicia, Adriana, Ree-Ree, Hanky, Kathy, and Karla.

I have a lot of family members on both sides that vary in age, where a lot of great, wonderful, joyful, and awesome memories were created over the years that helped shape a lot of the great moments I have experienced; I can't name them all but know I Love You All dearly and will cherish them for as long as I live and can remember (smile). This includes the numerous family members who have passed away.

Summertime also reminds me of the family vacations taken during summer breaks from school. I'm thankful as I think back on how well-rounded of an upbringing my parents exposed my brother and I to. Not only were summers spent with both sides of the family through our younger years, but we, as our own family unit, spent time together traveling to different places like Florida, Connecticut, Massachusetts, Georgia, Niagara Falls, Rye Play Land, Busch Gardens, staying in hotels, and timeshare homes, sometimes in the city and sometimes in the woods. It all shaped me and my preferences for what I wanted my own family to experience and create long-lasting memories for them.

With my own family, when I was married to Tyrone from Nacogdoches, Texas, we did a lot of entertaining wherever we were stationed when we were enlisted in the United States Air Force. We lived overseas for 11 years, bringing our children back to the states for their summers when we could, with time split between Nacogdoches, Texas, New York, and South Carolina. During our years in Germany, we bonded with Carl, Peaches, Dusty, Paco, Rob, Gary, Jennifer, Tiara, Nicolette, Tyrone, Helen, Dennis, Chanele, Devante, Ekesha, Mikey, and other families whose names escape me, but we would throw family gatherings and drive to other countries like Belgium, Italy through Switzerland, and Italy through Austria. We also camped in Austria, went to the Neuschwanstein Castle (Disney Logo), hosted many BBQs and various themed parties, and hiked through the vineyards. We went to the local carnivals that would set up in the nearby area where we lived. We also experienced the same type of activities when stationed in Misawa, Japan, where we participated in the festivals & parades with the locals. In addition, we went to amusement parks and enjoyed riding rides, playing games, and eating. We tried to immerse ourselves and our children in the culture. As I listen to my daughters, Jelisa and Tinisha, speak of their childhood during those years growing up overseas. They truly have memories upon which they think of very fondly along with the other military childhood friends they made during all our moves of where we lived (Germany twice, DC, Maryland, Virginia (aka DMV area twice), Japan, and United Kingdom.)

Last but not least for *"Pleasant Things"* are the memories and connections made with friends, families, and co-workers over my 24 Years of Service with the United States Airforce. There are so many people I have met during that time frame, who mean so much to me, it's impossible for me to list everyone, and I don't want to offend anyone by not mentioning them. So, I will say, if you knew me through deployments, gospel chapel services, community choir events, women's fellowships, bible studies, remote tours, participation in parades, carnivals, wine fest, Oktoberfest, indoor and outdoor concerts, comedy shows, etc... If you were stationed with me at Randolph AFB, San Antonio Texas; Kapaun Air Station, Germany; Pentagon, Washington DC; Osan Air Base, Korea; Ramstein Air Base, Germany; Misawa Air Base, Japan; RAF Lakenheath, England; Andrews Air Force Base, Maryland; along with the three times I deployed to Southwest Asia. Thank You, Thank You, Thank You, for all of you, who have been a part of my adult life at the start and what I have experienced from age 18 until I retired at 42! You are and will always be my Beloved Military Family, and I'm so thankful that even if we don't stay in contact often, we can keep in contact via social media, text message, and whenever we run into each other as we are now living our lives, it will always feel like a family reunion, making me smile from ear to ear and warming my heart and soul.

For the songs *Goodness of Christ* and *Living Christian,* my inspiration came from my time with Light of Glory

Ministry (aka LOGM.) This ministry was more than just a church experience; to me, we were more like a family. It was made up of a small congregation, but we did many great things and grew together. As with all families, there are some difficult moments to work through, we were not perfect and didn't always get things right, but we had a collective passion for God, Jesus, and the Holy Spirit. No matter what, we recognized the Authority of the Lord, always giving Him the Glory, Honor, and Praise.

Lifetime friendships were created within the ministry; in addition, we discovered ourselves, our gifts, and our strengths in who God said we were. We Praised, Worshipped, and Prayed to God no matter where our services were. When I joined, we were in a local community center, but it started out at the pastor's home with only 5 to 8 people, if I remember correctly. Then we went to an elementary school cafeteria, to a shopping center storefront that became our church home until the end of the ministry.

As mentioned in the Acknowledgements, our Praise and Worship team was something to be a part of. At times I felt our nights of preparation were better than our ministering in the Sunday service. The connection with the Holy Spirit is hard to explain, but you didn't want to come out of it, and it would be really late when we left, having to go to work the next morning. Which also led us to grow out of our comfort zone and under the encouragement of our pastor, who also learned how to play the piano and became our pianist, leading us to create our own Praise and Worship songs to minister on Sundays. Out of that experience is how I came to write the songs which are the basis of this book, *Seasoned by the Seasons of Grace.*

While serving at LOGM, we fellowshipped, served the community with gifts of food baskets, back to school bags & supplies, held community days, and had indoor services and outdoor services in the park with BBQs after service and nature walks. During my last military deployment, just before I rotated back home, God had spoken to me about starting an Intercessory Prayer Team, and He instructed me to talk with the pastor about creating one. Around the same time, we had a very powerful Prayer Circle, where the entire congregation would make one big circle around the room, and people spoke out loud about what their need was, and it was prayed for in the collective. God definitely heard and answered those prayers. During my first Sunday back at church after returning home, not having spoken to the pastor yet, he made an announcement about wanting to create an Intercessory Prayer Team because God had instructed Him to do so. Yup, that was the confirmation I experienced, and I wasn't even looking for it, but it taught me how to listen to what God says and how He will make it clear, what I perceived is truly from Him.

Another life-changing experience I had during my season on the Intercessory Prayer Team was the retreats we would go on once a quarter to different retreat centers. Again, it was another opportunity to experience a God moment that would renew our minds, bodies, and souls. In preparation, we would fast leading up to and sometimes during the retreat and break the fast together, either at the retreat center or at a restaurant on the way home. We would pray to start off, read scripture to fill ourselves with the Word of God, and then have special time alone time to hear from God. We each would go our separate ways with our journals and walk the grounds of the retreat centers and write down what God spoke to our spirits, what we observed in our surroundings, what was heard, and what was felt or even smelled. We then came back after the time we allotted ourselves and shared with one another what we had written and anything else God spoke.

It amazed me how sometimes we noticed the same things and described them in detail, but there were times when we had different perspectives on what we described, even though we were in the same environments, but at different times not consulting with one another but it all still being related and tying in together. For me, that experience answers the question I have heard people ask about why the Gospels of Matthew, Mark, Luke, and John give slightly different accountings of the same event they have witnessed during their season of walking with Christ.

At LOGM, we had various activities for the children to learn, experience, and grow in relationship with the Lord. They, too, created lifelong friendships as their parents did, which is still true to this day of me writing this book in 2022. We have witnessed the outdoor baptisms of many members, young and seasoned, in a pool, in the Potomac River in Virginia at Barnesfield Park, where a few times people who were driving across the Henry Nice bridge saw us and would beep their horns, then pause where they were headed to come to the part of the park where we were at, to watch or join in our service.

I will always be grateful and thankful to God for blessing my life with the growth that occurred during my time with my Light of Glory Ministries. I went from being like Martha, always busy inserting myself and doing anything I thought needed to be done, to being like Mary, learning at the feet of Jesus, and just doing those things God wanted me to do. God spoke that to me a couple of times, once during my last military deployment, and then He reminded me again through trusted friends. I realized I had blocked others from being able to take care of those same things that I wasn't supposed to do. So, with that seasoning, I must ensure I keep discernment of God, Christ, and the Holy Spirit being my focus in every aspect of my life.

Pleasant Things

[ADLIB at the end with just the music]:
Philippians 4:8 says, *"Finally, brothers and sisters, whatever is true, whatever is noble, whatever is right, whatever is pure, whatever is lovely, whatever is admirable—if anything is excellent or praiseworthy—think about such things."*

Chorus

I'll focus on
What's positive
and *Pleasant Things*
on *Pleasant Things*
(repeat)

Verse One

Just turned on the TV
to start watching the news
all I see is negativity

hate, turmoil, and the blues
All around the world, one group against another
sometimes, trouble found within
people not valuing the gift of life
Given by God, for our daily livin'

Verse Two

Keeping company with family and friends
with plenty of laughter and remember whens
grownups talking around the grill
while children are running and playing for thrills
music is blasting; there's singing and dancing
Everybody's smiling, fellowshipping and glancing
Full of God's joy and feeling grateful
These are the things that will keep your mind stable

Adlibs

There's just so much going on in this world, Things that want to tear you down, things and people who don't want to see you happy and joyous. But you have to discount all that stuff, and you just need to concentrate real hard and focus your mind with everything you have because nothing beats the peace that surpasses all understanding and that can only be

Seasoned by the Seasons of Grace
received from the one and only God and our Lord
and Savior Jesus Christ

Ending:

Focus on what's positive and *Pleasant Things, Pleasant Things, Pleasant Things,* Hold on tight to *Pleasant Things.*

Darlene D. Curl

Goodness of Christ

<u>*Chorus*</u>

When I think of the *Goodness of Christ*
and all the things He's done in my life
I sing glory (glory)
give Him honor (honor)
give Him Praise, Praise, Praise, Praise

<u>*Verse One*</u>

Time and Time again
You amaze me
My Lord, Savior, and Friend
You're my Provider
Jehovah Jireh
No one can compare to You

Your Love is like no other
By Grace and Mercy
and Blood we're covered

Seasoned by the Seasons of Grace

We don't even have to speak a word
for the thoughts, in our minds, by You can be heard

Verse Two

Even when
we go astray
You guide us back
to the path that You have paved
Your correction is more than fair
a chance for forgiveness and repentance through
prayer

Your goodness goes
beyond our physical
includes emotions, mental and spiritual
So, it's easy to give You the highest praise
Hallelujah for the rest of my days

Living Christian

__Chorus__

I love Jesus
I can't help it
I'm *Livin Christian*
and don't regret it
He saved my soul
Now I'm indebted
Yes, I love Jesus
I can't help it

__Verse One__

Yes, I am Bold
when I proclaim
my Love for Jesus
I am unashamed
Christ is worthy
of my claps and my shout

Seasoned by the Seasons of Grace

Not giving a chance
for the rocks to cry out

Verse Two

I'll testify
of all His goodness
who He is and
what He's done for me
I accept His guidance
His Disciplin
I want you to know
I really love me some Him

Read

Psalm 34:1-3;8-9

"I will bless the Lord at all times; His praise shall
continually be in my mouth. [2] My soul will make its boast
in the Lord; The humble will hear it and rejoice. [3] O
magnify the Lord with me And let us exalt His name
together.
[8] O taste and see that the Lord is good; How blessed is the
man who takes refuge in Him!
[9] O fear the Lord, you His saints; For to those who fear
Him, there is no want.

Intimate Reflections

Use this place to write your thoughts, a song, a poem, or something God has downloaded as you read through this Season and the accompanying songs.

Darlene D. Curl

Fall

D*uring* the Fall season, things start to change. It gets a little cooler, tree leaves start changing colors and fall, and there is a sense of preparation for something beautiful that is happening in the present. But also, something is about to take place that may not be so pleasant, depending on the perspective you choose to have. The next three songs created, *I Need You, Lord, Breathe in Me,* and *Walk in the Spirit,* are perfectly relatable to the Fall seasons of our lives. Below I share a personal reflection of what I experienced.

The life event I have chosen for the Fall representation is when I was unemployed from February to December 2017. I have worked since high school; I started out part-time at a clothing store called Anderson Little at the Newburgh Mall. I also worked at Friendly's restaurant and McDonald's before joining the United States Air Force under the delayed enlistment program my senior year of high school (Class of 1988). I served 24 years of Active Duty, and while on terminal leave, I started working as a contractor with the Department of Defense before my official retirement date of October

31, 2012. I worked on several contracts, and before each one would fully come to a close, even if it was just one or two days away from me not having a job, God saw fit for me to work in another position, and so I had no doubts in God being Jehovah Jireh (My Provider). I had never missed a paycheck from October 2012 to the end of January 2017. I had grown arrogant and took for granted that there was no way I wasn't going to get another job. I was caught up in the pattern of receiving another position as I always did in years prior.

[Pause in thought]

Now, as I am typing this part of my story, I'm reminded that I had that same thought process towards my promotion in the military. A few times when I made my next rank, right around the time, I was either about to change duty stations or had changed and found out in transition. Well, that wasn't the case when I tested for E-7, MSgt, it took a few years for me to achieve that rank, and when I did, *(whew)* it was at the transition of Winter going into Spring.

[Resuming]

Before my contract was up, I had started applying for other positions I knew I qualified for. However, when February rolled around, I hadn't found anything and didn't receive any calls for interviews. I applied for contracting jobs and government positions and even placed job applications in the private sector. I had friends and old co-workers who sent me job announcements for positions they knew I was a good fit for, but nothing was heard from the hiring managers. I even applied for jobs I was overqualified for, and I didn't receive any notifications. I tried thinking outside the box and looked at jobs I was familiar with but really didn't have any experience in because I started having a feeling of desperation, and yet there was still nothing.

By this time, it was summer, I still had no job, my savings was dwindling down, I had bills, and I had a trip to Costa Rica scheduled that I made sure was paid off before my position was up in January. I still needed to create and launch the website of my business and was able to do so. But I still hadn't received any job offers and was quite puzzled, because I just knew I should have received something by this time. I was still holding onto that thought of my past history of never missing a paycheck.

I remember attending one of LaKesha's Testimony parties at a church location during the week that I hadn't been to before. I shared how I didn't know what was going on; I didn't know why God was allowing this to take place, and that I wasn't feeling all that confident anymore. I was trying to stay faithful and trust in Him, but it was tough doing so when the bill collectors were asking for payments that I didn't have. Thankfully, I at least had my military retirement to at least pay the mortgage. I prayed that I would get an understanding of what God was trying to reveal to me. This isn't like me to be in this position, I had my plans, but God's plan always trumps ours. As stated in Jeremiah 29:11, *"For I know the plans and thoughts that I have for you,' says the Lord, 'plans for peace and well-being and not for disaster, to give you a future and a hope."*

I have been told on many occasions that I am a giver, whether it's my time, energy, financial blessings, food, clothes, rides, a place to stay, etc. During this Fall season of life, what God was showing and getting me to see, was a new thing that needed to be worked into my life and awareness. I wasn't a good receiver of people's kindness, help, or assistance in situations where I needed to be submissive and receive instead of becoming defensive, assertive, and doing all the time. I had friends that gave me assistance, even though my initial response was no; I can't accept that, to me being scolded about not taking what they were offering without it being an argument but eventually giving in. I believe that due to my singleness, I have had to rely on myself to get things accomplished, and that has played a big part in my way of thinking.

I had a friend that I sang in the choir with when I was stationed in the United Kingdom at RAF Lakenheath named Mary. At this point, it had been a few years since I had heard or spoken to her, but in the midst of going through what was happening, I received a call from her. At first, we delighted in having the opportunity to speak to one another, but what I didn't know, and what I have come to learn; is that it was a God moment that was about to rock my world and bring about change. After exchanging pleasantries,

Mary asked me what was going on because God had placed me on her mind heavily.

[Pause in Thought]

I have come to the knowledge that whenever Mary calls me, it's because God is using her to get my attention about something. When God has placed someone on your mind, you need to reach out to that person; however you can, regardless of how much time or what has passed between the two of you, because He is using you for His purpose.

[Resuming]

So, I shared with her what was going on, and that I did not understand the why, because I was doing what I thought I was supposed to be doing, I am normally on top of things, and I pay my bills on time. I have the perspective that I don't want to impose on people, and I didn't want to become a burden to anyone. She said, *"I'm going to stop you right there,"* and asked me, *"do you hear what you have been saying?" "I this, and I that, there seems to be an awful lot of "I" being talked about but what about God?"* She said, *"If you are in need of help and assistance, why haven't you asked?"* I told her I didn't want to be an imposition on anyone. She stated that it's more about your pride than anything else, and you aren't a good receiver.

She went on to say; I remember you being a wonderful giver of yourself, but sometimes, givers are awful receivers when it's their turn. She said you are in a season where you must learn to be a gracious receiver as much as you are a giver. She said, when you have figured that out, that's when things will start to turn around for you. I listened to what she said and didn't believe or accept it at first until a few more of my close friends said the same things Mary said, about me having prideful ways, because I didn't reach out to ask for help.

I started seeking God in prayer, and during my quiet times I spent with Him, talking but mostly listening, I finally realized what was said and told to me.

[Pause in thought]

When I say I hear from God, I don't hear an actual voice, but it's more so the manner in which thoughts come to my mind. Some people say it is their subconscious or a gut feeling, but I believe it's God, in the form of the Holy Spirit, who dwells within each believer that has confessed Jesus Christ as their Lord and Savior.

[Resuming]

They also stated that I was blocking their blessings by not allowing them to help me out. So, it then became clear to me that the reason why I hadn't found a new job was because there were things God had to work out of me and become empty in order to receive the fullness and overflow of what He had for me. Once He shifted my thought process of what I thought it meant for Him to be my Keeper and Provider. Through what I experienced and how I experienced it in its totality, I came to a new understanding of what it means to be reliant upon Him. However, He does things, whomever He uses to carry out those things, and trusting Him while it's happening (the part we don't necessarily get to see) is what leads us to the results of

His provisions for us. After He saw that I genuinely received and understood what He was teaching me, He set things in motion for me to be sent a job offer in November of 2017 that would have my start date begin in December 2017, and my drought was over. A couple of updates to this story to bring it to the current status can be found in the Spring section of this book.

I Need You Lord

Chorus

Lord
I need you, Lord
Cause I don't know
Which way to go

Verse One

Strong one
That's what people say
When they see me living my life
Smiling each and every day
Truth be told
I'm masking misery and strife
My inside is not reflected outside
Cause I'm not alright

Verse Two

Dealing

When you’re caught off guard
Trying to keep it all together has become really hard
Deciding
How do I proceed on
making right decisions
praying that I don't choose wrong

Verse Three

I surrender
now vulnerable to You
exposing myself completely, totally open to You
No more pretending
I'm going to take the time
To connect with You depend on You
Heal my body, soul, and mind

Ending

Lord, I need You in my life
When I’m awake and asleep at night
Never be a time when I won’t need You
Without You Lord what would I do

Breathe In Me

Beginning

Each and every day
During the circumstances of life
When things seem to be against me
bringing me grief and strife

Which weighs me down
and looking for relief
but it cannot be found
because it can only be breathed

Verse

Breath in Me
Lord
Fill me with
Your
Majesty
Oh Lord

Darlene D. Curl

Breath it in me

Spiritually

Your

Divinity

Last

Eternally

Oh Lord

Breath it in me

Adlibs

Love

Joy

Peace

Kindness

Favor

Grace

Mercy

Truth

Patience

Wisdom

Trust

Strength

Seasoned by the Seasons of Grace

2nd Adlibs

Discernment

Encouragement

Endurance

Hope

Knowledge

Healing

Restoration

Faith

Righteousness

Gentleness

New Life

Victory

Ending

Revive my mind
Revive my soul
Revive my heart
Make me whole

Revive my body
It belongs to you
Breath into me
That I may be renewed

Darlene D. Curl

All those things

that comes from you

Breathe

Walk In the Spirit

Intro

First Corinthians 10:13

"No temptation has overtaken you except what is common to mankind. And God is faithful; he will not let you be tempted beyond what you can bear. But when you are tempted, he will also provide a way out so that you can endure it."

Chorus

Walk in the Spirit
Don't let flesh take over
Deny your desires
Or risk of harmful exposure
Present your body
As a living sacrifice
Holy, Acceptable to Jesus Christ

<u>Verse One</u>

I'm having impure thoughts
Invading my mind
I want to feel really good and satisfied
My wildest desires and fantasies
That would bring much pleasure
To this human body

<u>Verse Two</u>

I want to do right
I try to be good
My actions are opposite of
doing what I should
Even with the knowledge
Of a price to be paid
The seduction of temptation
Has my flesh engaged

<u>Verse Three</u>

God said
I won't be tempted
Beyond what I am able
He's true to His Word
And He's always faithful

Seasoned by the Seasons of Grace

So, when the tug of war happens
Between my flesh & spirit
God, I need my escape
Am I anywhere near it?

<u>*Single Mother*</u>

<u>Chorus</u>

She is special
and made like no other
The children in her home
They call her mother
Further distinction
She's doing it alone
A single mother
Is how she is known
Single mother, single mother, single mother

<u>Verse One</u>

Bone of his bone
Flesh of his flesh
God created woman
To be a man's help
From the beginning
She was set apart

Seasoned by the Seasons of Grace

Created from the bone, protecting
his breath and beat of his heart

__Verse Two__

Circumstances of her life
She's not married, not a wife
whether by choice or a life event
It doesn't discount who she represents
She sacrifices in ways you don't know
for food and clothing and a place to call home
Sometimes feeling like a failure
Losing breaths like she needs an inhaler

__Verse Three__

Now, this fact that should be said
She has a God that isn't dead
The earth is His, and the fullness thereof
Provided for by family and friends with love
She is strong, smart, and able
and with the Lord, she's more than capable
overcoming the negative strife
that people will try to speak into her life

Darlene D. Curl

Adlibs

It's not an easy task to raise a child on your own, but it is possible when you have the right support system in place. Like the "*it takes a village to raise a child approach,*" you define who will be a part of the village. If you follow God's lead, He will put you on the path to connect with good people that will have the means to assist you. Or even if they are in the same set of circumstances as you, join together and take care of each other, then you will be taken care of. I thank God for my family and friends, who have been a true Blessing to me over the years when I became a...*Single Mother.*

Intimate Reflections

Winter

D*uring* the Winter season, things seem harsh and hard to handle. It can feel like you can't catch a break because one thing after another seems to happen and take place. Everyone goes through issues that can wear us down and bring us to the point of depression, despair, crying out for help, and looking for someone, anyone, to give us assistance with the hurt, pain, and suffering felt. On top of how we have become, we are skillful and creative in mastering the art of wearing a mask so no one can detect when something is not right with us. Often in today's society, there is a lack of empathy, human decency, common sense, and compassion for people and life itself. You really don't know what a person is going through, dealing with, and/or have already dealt with. Especially if you haven't taken the time to get some sort of understanding about them, given the details or not. This is one reason why we should show kindness in how we talk to people, how we relate to people, and how we may even view people. I've read statistics that talk about some of life's great stressors that people can face at a time. I know I'm not the first, last, or only person to have experienced major life losses of separation/divorce, death of a loved one, and having to be separated from your loved ones while trying to make sense and dealing with all of that, one after another, just in one season of life. This is my Winter season, which I thought would best go with the songs written, *The Struggle is Real, Betrayal,* and *Comfort Me.*

The most difficult time of my life was 2006 when I was serving in the United States Air Force, stationed in the United Kingdom, going through separation without letting any of my family members know. Lying, saying he was working, asleep, out running errands, or in the bathroom, when they would call and ask where my husband was so, they could say hello. I pretended all was still good; I kept up the charade by even having my children pretend all was okay when interacting with my family living in the states. Even with them, I didn't go into the details of why the separation took place; what I was concerned about for them was not to poison their minds with the hurt, pain, and emotional suffering I was going through. Whatever they thought of their father was going to be based upon their own dealings and relationship with him. I also didn't want to jade them from having a positive relationship of their own in the future when they became adults. So, I sacrificed outward displays of my displeasure and internalized it all.

God revealed what was going on to my friend and Sister in Christ, Tracy, from the Gospel Service at the Chapel at RAF Lakenheath, and she questioned me about it in the parking lot in front of the Chapel. I still remember it clear as day; I got out of my car as we were headed toward the building to go in for Sisterhood; it was Tracy, Sis Dixon, Chaplain Dixon's wife, and Mary. Tracy stopped, looked up in the sky towards the Lord, and said, *"Sis, God wants me to ask you what's going on with you."* At first, I said nothing, but she was insistent because God was insisting upon her that I speak to her. Eventually, I shared that I was going through a separation, I didn't go into the details but shared that it had started the previous year, and they could tell I wasn't in a good place mentally, emotionally, and spiritually; I had become weak.

During this time, my father had come out of remission from his battle with bladder cancer, which was diagnosed six or seven years previously. He endured several operations, radiation, and chemotherapy treatments during those years. I was planning on bringing my daughters to the states for their spring break in April of 2006 to visit with my parents. After being in the hospital undergoing a procedure to try to slow down cancer that had metastasized to other parts of his body, I remember receiving a phone call from my mother, telling me if I was still planning on coming home for spring break, that I shouldn't wait that long because my father was being released from the hospital to hospice care. My heart broke even more because I was truly a daddy's girl; we had the same type of humorous personality, cracking jokes, laughing, and doing funny and silly things like how my paternal grandmother (Katherine) was. In my eyes, Mom was more serious, stern, and the disciplinarian (traits I didn't really come to appreciate until I reached my 30s).

[Pause in Thought]

Quick flashback story as it was told to me, both my parents were previously married, and neither had children with their former spouses. My father was told that he couldn't have children during that marriage. Then years later, when he and my mom met through my paternal grandmother (she and my mom were both nurses at the VA hospital in Montrose, NY) and started dating, he was still under the belief he couldn't have children, well, let's just say I proved all that wrong.

[Resuming]

I told my mom it was going to take a red cross message from my father's doctor for me to be able to take emergency leave back to the states, for which I had a maximum of 30 days that would be authorized. I remember having to go to my daughters' schools to get them released as soon as the travel arrangements were made by my first sergeant to go home to Newburgh, New York. I contacted my spouse to tell him the news, and we agreed not to say anything about our separation situation because I was afraid it would make my father's health deteriorate faster. We told the girls what was going on and asked them not to say anything to anyone as well about our living arrangements.

Once we arrived at my parents' home, we assisted my mom with the care of my Dad when the hospice nurse wasn't there. I remember my paternal grandmother, who only lived 45 min away in Howells, NY, near Middletown, NY, had someone bring her over to the house. In hindsight, I wished I had thought about recording this visit because anytime my father and his mother got together or even talked on the phone, it was a laugh-fest for sure. She, being around 89 years old, and my father 73 years old, was trying to get him to eat cause, at this point, his appetite was starting to go. She told me what I needed to buy and fix for him to get his strength back, and them arguing back and forth about he was too old for her to tell him what to do and how he still towered over her at 6'2," and her around 5'1 and she can't push him around.

Each day I watched my father become less active, not hungry, not thirsty, and seeing people around him that we didn't see, talking in a language unknown to us and reliving and making gestures of tasks he did when he was in the Navy in his younger days. It was brought to my remembrance how God had already prepared me for this season of what I was witnessing. It was through what was told to me by my mother-in-law years before that, as she watched her mother transition from life to death, and I remembered everything. After about a week and a half, my oldest daughter Jelisa and my spouse had to go back to the United Kingdom because she had standardized tests to take for school (which she has expressed the regret of having to leave), and he had to get back to work. I remember the exchange of words between my father and Jelisa as she was brushing her long hair (she has his hair texture) in the mirror in my parents' bedroom, where he became immobile. He apologized to her because he would not be around to see her graduate from high school in the following year. They exchanged I love you's and the look of pride he had on his face at seeing his granddaughter when he thought he couldn't even have children at one point in his life still brings tears to my eyes.

My brother made it to NY from Atlanta, GA, where he was a military police officer after getting out of the Army at Ft McPherson with his two boys, Devon and Salomon. We had a gathering of family, friends, and a few of the AME Zion Church family members I grew up with at my parent's house. We had a good time, but it was a lot of stimulation for my father. Even though he was immobile, in the middle of the night, after all the excitement of the people who came to visit and spend time with the family, I heard my mom saying Henry, what are you doing? What's going on with you? Keep still. My old bedroom where I was staying was right next to theirs, and I found out later that morning that my dad was swinging his legs around back and forth. That was the last burst of energy the body gives towards the last couple of days, as though the person has made a recovery and must be getting stronger.

My brother was leaving to drive back to Atlanta this day, and I remember being in the kitchen with my nephews while my brother said his goodbyes. My mom came down the stairs with tears in her eyes, telling me what was said. Upon my brother saying, *"Okay, Dad see you on the next trip up,"* my father told him, *"No, this is it. There won't be a next time."* So, I went upstairs and got my camera, and I asked my brother to get close to our father so that I could take their picture. I walked my brother and nephews outside to their car and watched them drive off. I then wanted a picture with my father, and within just a few minutes of taking a picture of my father and brother together, compared to the picture I took with my father, you can physically see that my father had concluded all that he needed to. He was still alive, but there was a difference in his appearance. I sat with my father with the TV on, holding his hand at times, checking on him to make sure he was comfortable, and laying my head on his shoulder.

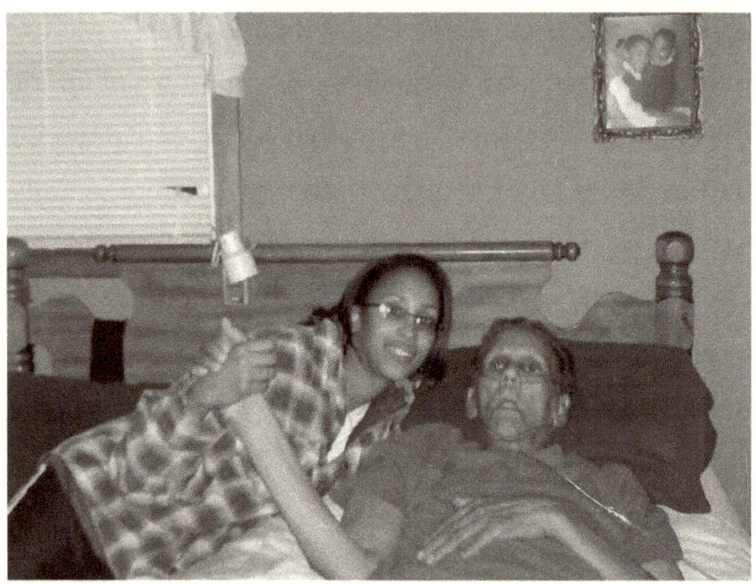

Two days later, I remember my mom waking me up in the morning by saying, *"Darlene, if you want to say goodbye to your father, now is the time to do it."* I was still half asleep until it clicked what was happening, and I jumped up out of bed so fast that I fell on my knee. I woke up my youngest daughter Tinisha and told her what was happening, and we went into my parents' bedroom. My mom had one of his hands, and I went to the other side of the bed and picked up his other hand and held it as I told him how much I loved him and how great of a father he was, and how I would miss him. Tinisha looked at him, touched his hand, and said, *"I love you, Poppy."*

I called my brother while still sitting next to my father and told him how our father had begun his transitioning. Dexter asked me to tell our father what was on his heart, and I did just that, like a bridge making the connection of messages (this is so relevant in so many ways in my life), not only from my brother but my spouse, my grandmother (Katherine) who wanted to be there but couldn't find anyone to bring her at the time, and then finally my parents' Pastor, Rev Twila Cains. As I was telling my father all the messages of love from the people who cared for him, I felt him squeeze my hand ever so lightly to let me know that he was still there and present and heard everything that I had said. I kissed his cheek when I heard the doorbell. Rev Cains arrived at the house, mom stayed in the bedroom, and after I opened the front door for Pastor Cain to come into the house, I cried in her arms before she went upstairs to give my dad his last rites.

I couldn't go back upstairs; instead, I went into the garage by myself to continue to cry, and mom told me when Rev Cains was done, dad breathed his last breath, and his chest rose no more. I called the hospice nurse to tell her of my father's passing, and she came and cleaned up his body. My grandmother eventually found someone to bring her to the house, and when I assisted her up to the bedroom, she collapsed on top of my father, crying and saying what was in her heart, but he had already gone.

A couple of hours later, Mr. Rhodes, the coroner, who knew both of my parents, was called, and he came and got my father. I remember Mr. Rhodes instructing me to have everyone gathered in the dining room to look away from the stairs leading from the bedroom because he didn't want them to have the memory of seeing him being removed from the house in a body bag on the gurney. But I watched everything, including my father being loaded into the hearse and driving off. I even went to my neighbors who knew my family that I had grown up around and told them of the news.

I stayed another two weeks to help my mom, make the arrangements, call family, and receive family at the house for the funeral a week later. I even sang during his service a song called *Well Done My Child* by the Nelons. Family from both my dad's and mom's side came, it's sad to think that you only get to see some people during these types of occasions, but it was still good to see everyone.

One of my mom's sisters, Aunt Claudia, stayed with mom for a few days, which was good because I had to make my way back to the UK to my duty station because my 30 days were about up. However, being home for almost 30 days, I didn't realize I wasn't taking care of myself while assisting in the caretaking of my dad for the two weeks leading up to his death and then helping my mom with what I could, the two weeks after. I wasn't really big, to begin with; I think I was around 125 pounds, very slender, but on the morning before the day I was leaving, I got a glimpse of myself in the mirror; before stepping into the shower, I scared myself with what I saw. My eyes had sunken into my skull, my bone structure was really pronounced, and I did not look healthy at all. After weighing myself, I had dropped 20 pounds during that time frame of being home. I realized that in taking care of everyone else, I neglected myself but didn't feel it, but God made me see it once things were somewhat under control.

When I returned to the UK, I was told it was very obvious I didn't take care of myself, and the people I knew and who cared rallied around me to ensure I started to, especially my RAF Lakenheath Chapel Family! After that experience, I realized the gift I was given; I witnessed the actual homegoing of my earthly father to our Heavenly Father while holding his hand as he lay in his bed peacefully, in his own home, and if you were wondering, my father passed away not knowing that his daughter was going through a separation!

Then, in July of 2006, while in my office at work, my supervisor and I were having a conversation when my cellphone rang, and it was my sister-in-law, Kersha. She asked me if I was sitting down, and I immediately thought, *"Oh God did something happen to my mother,"* and she told me that my brother had passed away at work from a heart attack. My brother was 30 years old, five years younger than I, our father had just passed away three months prior, and I was dazed. I didn't realize it but, I just started walking out of my office, trying to make sense of what I was being told, when my supervisor gently directed me back into my office, shut my door, and went to tell our commander, and the first sergeant so we could start the process of getting me back to states again.

My unit, the 493rd Fighter Squadron crew, was the best in taking care of my family and me. Having to call the schools again and call my spouse, whom I was still separated from, but my main concern was that no one told my mom while she was at work. From the VA hospital to where she lives, she had to drive around Bear Mountain, which is a really windy road and can be challenging with a clear mind and good road conditions. Mom was still mourning my father, and now she has to be told that her only son is gone too!

I am all the way in the UK. Not having time to grieve or get sad because I knew I was going to have to be strong for my mom. I called my brother's Godparents, my older cousins Gene and Margret, and told them the news. I asked them to go to mom's house to wait on her to get home from work and let her know because of the time difference and wanting someone there with her. Mom was late getting home because she had gone to the HR office that very day to change her emergency

contact information and other paperwork from my father to my brother since I was stationed overseas, and he could be easily reached. When I called to see if mom had been told, I heard her wailing (I never knew what that meant until that moment) in the background as I spoke to my cousin. I told them we were making our way to come back, and so my family stepped up and stepped in, taking care of my mom until I got there. My sister-in-law's family was taking care of her and my nephews, so I was able to concentrate on mom.

I was numb, but not to the point of letting myself go as I did the months previously with my father's passing. I assisted when and where I was asked to be of help. I mainly had to put all my time and energy into helping out my mom and was able to be home again for another 30 days of emergency leave. Remember when I stated that my mom was the strong one and the disciplinary and serious parent during my years of living at home? Now, I had to see my mom in a broken state, which didn't seem at all possible in young Darlene's eyes, but as an adult Darlene, being a mom of 2 children, I understood and became really concerned for my mom. What was I going to do when it was time for me to go back overseas? It was almost too much to bear.

[Pause in Thought]

What I haven't shared is that I had a few moments where I almost blacked out or passed out, from suppressing my emotions to be strong for my mom when she needed me most. When it comes to her and her wellbeing, I will do it all over again, no matter what; as long as I have breath, and the God-given strength within me, I will take care of my Mom (I Love you, Veronica, oops I mean Mom).

[Resuming]

God answered my concerns when a win-win situation arose in the midst of this family tragedy. My sister-in-law moved in with my mother for a while. She and some of her cousins went down to Atlanta, cleared her out of her apartment, and drove a U-Haul back to New York with their belongings. A miracle occurred in this story, Kersha's cousin, who was driving the U-Haul truck, had a blown-out tire with tread missing but was able to drive all the way to the house and didn't even realize the condition of the tire. I took a picture of it because that was nothing but a miracle that he didn't get into an accident. We converted my old bedroom into a room for my nephews, who were 5 and 7 years old at the time. Kersha stayed in my brother's old bedroom, and, in case you were wondering again, my brother passed away, not knowing that his sister was going through separation while dealing with the death of our father!

After I returned back to the United Kingdom in July of 2006, in September of that same year, I had to deploy for a second time and couldn't get released from going. I tried, my leadership tried and was told they were sorry, but I still had to go.

Seasoned by the Seasons of Grace

In hindsight, my personal walk with the Lord has taught me that I had to go because it was a God-ordained four-month deployment. I went from knowing of God, Jesus Christ, and the Holy Spirit to having a deep and meaningful relationship with the Trinity as I saw and experienced many spiritual events I'd only read about and was skeptical of prior to going! During this time, God used me in many ways that I wasn't aware of. For example, my friend Crystal shared with me in our last phone conversation towards the end of 2021 how she was going through her own personal battles and said she was just going to attend the church services but not be involved in the ministry. However, for both of us, God had His plans, and He linked us both up together because He used both of us to be a help to one another in our spiritual walks in different ways that complimented the other. Crystal said she would often look at me in amazement after all that I had been through in 2006 and shared how amazed she was to see me do what I had to do to get close to God, praising Him even in the office.

Crystal was my office mate who I became close friends with during that deployment in 2006, along with our friends Q, Joy, and Travia. We both were called to be participants in the ministry to do things at the chapel. When I questioned, "Why me?" because I am not qualified for any of that, and what made the people in leadership even consider me in the first place? The answer was always God placed me upon their hearts and thoughts to be a part of what was going on.

One of the experiences I had was when I was a part of the early bird prayer team (it was called something else, but I can't remember the name). I had almost forgotten about being connected to a prayer team back then, upon which I experienced some memorable things that are coming back to me as I am typing.

A prayer wall was created in the chapel, and simply, anybody could come in, write their issue and/or prayer request on a sticky note anonymously and place it on the wall for people who believed in the power of prayer to pray over the request written. There was one morning that I went in for morning prayer and went to the wall; as I was reading over the request, there was one particular one that stood out to me, it was a woman in a similar situation as me, whose marriage had failed, and she wanted God to give her guidance. So, I decided to pay over her request, but what was unexpected to me was as I closed my eyes and placed my hand on her note, I felt a pulse of energy leave out of my body through my fingertips to that note before I even uttered a word. It was the strangest sensation I had ever felt, but I couldn't let it distract me from my prayer and did so.

Later on, that evening, we had bible study, and I spoke to one of the instructors, told her what took place earlier that morning, and asked what happened. She told me I experienced something like what Jesus felt when the woman with the issue of blood touched the hem of his garment, and some of his anointing was transferred to her to heal her of her issue. But instead of someone touching me and taking the anointing out of me, when I did the touching, it was being given through me. I don't know what if anything happened in that woman's life because there wasn't a name written as I remember, but I remember the instructor asking me if I prayed over myself to replenish what had left out of me, and I said no, that I didn't know I was supposed to and so she did. To ensure that anything that was not of God didn't get a chance to take up the space left by the anointing leaving me. At the time, it was strange and confusing, but in this present day, as I am typing. I have a better understanding of what happened and the actions and words of the instructor.

When I got back to the UK from my deployment in the desert, Tracy shared with me that all that I had experienced in my Season of 2006 was going to quickly advance me in my growth, for what was required of me in my walk and journey with the Lord and it has. The worst of my Winter Season in 2006 prepared me and taught me how to persevere through so much and showed me just how tough and strong I am with the Lord, and showed others, what is possible for them to endure and go through to become an Overcomer!

I'd also like to add this interesting fact that nn October 8, 2015 I posted the following on FaceBook: When I saw a post from Tyler Perry's page this morning, I was on an emotional roller coaster of being Wowed, to sadness, to Joy. What an accomplishment to go from being homeless in trying to make your dreams come true, never giving up, and to see the fruition of your labor even though it was many years later, and then to be in a position to purchase a base that was closed down, ensuring you have a place of your own to further your projects etc...Until I realized that is the base where my brother collapsed and died at work, then tears of sadness welled in my eyes as the story of what happened replayed in my mind from what I was told, and how one of the guard shacks was named after him "Robinson Station," up until the base closed down...But then I think about how I enjoy all the laughter talent and happiness that Tyler has in his projects and how that will replace the sad memory of what took place for my family, with more pleasant thoughts about what will be created, and produced at that location!

POLICE
DEPARTMENT OF THE ARMY
UNITED STATES OF AMERICA
1646
DIRECTORATE OF EMERGENCY SERVICES
POLICE STATION
FORTS MCPHERSON AND GILLEM

POLICE
DEPARTMENT OF THE ARMY
UNITED STATES OF AMERICA
1646
POLICE STATIO

ROBINSON STATION
POLICE

The Future Home of
Tyler Perry
Studios

Struggle is Real

Chorus

The struggle is real
The stress that I feel
No longer concealed
The struggle is real

Verse One

I've heard it said in Mathew 6, and verse 34
tomorrow has its own troubles; what are you worrying for
then I heard that struggle will make us strong as we grow
but there are days when I feel like I just can't take any more

Verse Two

Just because you're a child of the most high God

Seasoned by the Seasons of Grace
Doesn't mean we're exempt from the issues that life presents
Feeling every emotion that can be found from within
You reach a point in your life where you can no longer pretend

Verse Three

Ephesian 6 verse 12 says we fight not against flesh and blood
but dark and spiritual forces in the heavenly realms
Which means that we can't handle all life problems alone
So, call on the name that can make things change, Jesus our Lord

Ending

The struggle is real
the stress that I feel
I make my appeal
Humbly I Kneel

Betrayal

<u>Intro</u>

The definition of Betrayal – is the breaking or violation of trust, or confidence, that produces moral and psychological conflict within relationships of individuals, organizations, and businesses.

It is written in Luke 21:16, *"You will be betrayed even by parents, brothers and sisters, relatives and friends, and they will put some of you to death."* Betrayal, How do you handle it?

<u>Chorus</u>

How to recover
from the loss of trust
from deception
How do you get beyond
being shattered into a thousand pieces

Seasoned by the Seasons of Grace

Verse One

Imagine a story, a tale of betrayal
containing broken hearts and depression
but it's not fiction; it's so very real
wondering, if you can ever heal?

Verse Two

Anyone and everyone
Touched and affected by
Betrayal occurring in our lives
Professionally with family and friends

Verse Three

We're told how to handle this thing
by the example of our Savior and King
Jesus was betrayed and crucified
but said Father, "forgive them" before He died

Verse Four

The power of forgiveness
is the first step in how you can begin
Like how the Blood of our Savior covers up our past sins
Healing can begin when forgiveness is attained

allowing peace to increase and the ceasing of the pain

<u>Written Speaking Part</u>

Again, I ask you, how do you handle betrayal? Have you tried forgiveness? To do so means we release the offender and the offense committed against us, which in turn releases us from the burden of carrying that heavyweight. It's important to remember that forgiveness is not given because a person deserves it, but instead, it is an act of love, mercy, and grace. Christ showed us how, on the Cross, God says, "*We must forgive in order to be forgiven.*"

Forgiveness is the Key.

We can then move forward and not be burdened by strife

Being lifted to a whole new level, with Jesus Christ, and live your life

You have the victory in Jesus

<u>Recorded Speaking Part</u>

That is one way of How you can battle against betrayal. Don't let it bring you down. Don't have it take you to a place like a deep dark hole, you can't climb out of.

There is hope, regardless of the hurt that you feel or the anger that may build up inside. There is a more positive way of fighting against feelings of the fire you feel of being betrayed.

Forgiveness is the Key!

Forgiveness is the Key!

Comfort Me

Intro

During certain times in our lives

We are going to have some stuff happen and go through

And those things are capable of bringing us down to a point

Where we are feeling tired, beat down, and blue

However, we should not give up but recognize we need some help

Get with God, one on one, and know with Him you can always be yourself

Chorus

Comfort me

Lord, my soul, is low

Lord, please hear this song

Oh Lord, *comfort me*

I can't take no more

Seasoned by the Seasons of Grace

Lord, I really need your strength

Verse One

God, I'm seeking Ye first
Your kingdom and your righteousness
Just as Matthew 6:33 says to do
Feeling like I'm in a whirlwind
That is tossing me from here to there
Holding on by a thread, too much for me to bear

Verse Two

Needing to feel your warm embrace
Wanting You to take away the heartache, hurt, and pain
Desiring for everything to be right again
I know it's just a matter of time
A season in which to go through
Console me, encourage me as only You can do

Intimate Reflections

Spring

Spring can be a representation of things being reborn, renewed, having new experiences, and new opportunities. For this section, I'm choosing to share about the various experiences that have occurred and updates to what was shared during the other seasons of my life that are a complement to the songs of *Lord You Are* (the only song that was digitally mastered, registered, and released for purchase), *Grounded,* and *God is in Control.*

In 2014 instead of buying Christmas gifts for my close friends, I decided to make them something homemade. So, I looked at some YouTube videos about what kind of homemade gifts I could create and saw some that showed how to make body butter crème. After creating the gifts, which were going to be a one-and-done thing, two of my friends, Lisa H. and Stella, liked the products so much that they kept asking for more for over a year. Sometime in 2015, Stella then told me of how a co-worker of hers kept using her butter. She told the lady to contact me to get her own jar. She did contact me, and she stated that she would pay me for it.

I asked the Lord in prayer if there was something to this. After which, I started to hear messages about creating a business. At church, the story of Elisha and the widowed woman was the message on Sunday after I asked the Lord my question. Elisha instructed the woman to use the oil she had in her home to create income to pay off the debts she was left with upon the death of her husband, so I also started sharing samples in condiment cups with people at my job to get their opinion, and they liked it and said they would support the idea of me selling it. People then started sharing information about creating a business without me prompting them for it first.

I had a conversation with my friend LaShanda and LaKesha at different times because they both were already entrepreneurs, and they allowed me to ask questions to get things started. When I submitted the application to the State of Maryland, they officially created my business and company on April 25, 2016. When I mentioned my product to my friend George, who is a massage therapist, he utilized my body butter on his clients for about a year and a few of his clients became clientele of mine. My goal is always to create and provide natural and healthy skincare products. I strive to make a difference by using fresh, quality ingredients while putting prayer, energy, time, and effort into the processing of each product created from the batches. However, the most important part of my business I want to be made known is that it was Divinely Inspired and Purposed by God.

Its creation goes beyond the products and the company. It's a ministry involving crossing paths and making connections with people through simple conversations, making myself available to just listen to what's being shared, sometimes sharing my own testimonies to encourage their own purpose and dreams, to assist financially, or create networking opportunities. I remain open to having me or my business used by God as He sees fit. I have already witnessed and experienced these kinds of encounters many times over the five years I have been in business.

Even though I spoke of 2017 as having been my Fall Season of life, there were a couple of experiences that had a Spring Vibe in the midst of everything that transpired. While I was not working, I had the opportunity to join and work out at the 9Rounds Cardio Kickboxing studio in Waldorf, Maryland, owned by Wanda, aka Boss, and run by her Niece aka Honey Bee. I was given the name Bicep Curl. I was still going on my Costa Rica trip in the early fall of 2017 with the meet-up group called Grown & Sexy 40+, and I wanted to be in shape and look good in a bikini. I was able to attend the sessions five days out of the week, which started in May. I began seeing some of the same people around the time I attended and became friends with Chaves, Special K, Warrior, JJ Strong, Alex, Philly, River, and Butter Pecan. I made new friends, and I was able to get into the shape I wanted to be in within my five-month goal.

What also assisted me with meeting and exceeding my goal, after my 9Round workout routine, I had the opportunity to take long nature walks on a daily basis on the Indian Head Trail. It was my alone time connecting with God, listening to the sounds of the animals rustling in the woods and taking a peek at me walking by, feeling the breeze blowing on a windy day, feeling the warmth on my face and skin. The peace I felt during this time was something that brought me great Joy.

There were days that I would have great conversations with the Lord and would be out there for hours, not caring about the time or the problems and issues I was dealing with. I saw a lot of deer and beavers, heard the frogs, saw and heard the birds, all kinds of insects flying around or making their particular noises. I set goals for how far out I would go and how long I would walk. One day I felt so good that I just kept walking, forgetting that I needed to turn around to walk back to my car; by the time I finished, my feet were screaming because I had walked a half marathon (13 Miles) without training to build up to it. After that walk, it took me a few days to recover, but what an experience I had, and I survived!

Another wonderful Spring season I experienced in 2017 was with my business Daily Desire LLC. Which actually was created and established the previous year on April 25th, 2016. Starting the business in faith, believing this is what God had inspired me to create, I started to learn what it meant to become an entrepreneur, starting off with creating homemade body butter only at first, growing and expanding to creating other Skincare Products, that started originally as Christmas gifts two years prior in December 2014.

In August of 2017, my friend Lisa H. invited me to attend the two-day Ubiquitous Hair, Health and Beauty Expo at the Washington DC Convention center. The Saturday we went, we did a lot of walking around trying to take in as many of the vendor booths we could, along with the Hip Hop Entertainment, guest speakers, Celebrity product sales, and specialized sessions with company reps of the products we have grown accustomed to buying and hear about.

We had a great time and made a mental note of what vendor we were going to visit on Sunday when we came back. So, upon our return, we took our time at the booths we visited. We stopped at a booth that was selling eyelashes and had some applied. Afterward, we walked towards the stage area where people had started to gather to see the Gospel Artist that was on the lineup. As we found a spot to stand, Lisa stated she saw the Expo's creator, Germaine walking towards our way. So, the next thing I knew, she stopped next to me and said hello, beautiful, I love your lashes; I thanked her and stated that I loved the color of her shirt, and funny enough, we were wearing the same color, a hot fuchsia pink.

She then asked me what I thought about the expo and what it was that I did and I told her that I was there because my friend Lisa had asked me to join her to attend and we were just taken back by how wonderful an expo it was. I told her I wasn't currently working, but I had started a business last year, making body butter, and had just launched my website a couple of months prior.

Germaine asked me why wasn't I a vendor at the event. I informed her I was just starting out; I didn't know about the expo, and I wasn't currently working and didn't know about being a vendor. She told me to make sure I spoke with her manager Kathy to add my contact information to her list to contact. Germaine proceeded to tell me that I was missing out on a blessing not being there. She told me to do whatever I needed to do to be a vendor at the expo the next year in 2018, and even though I wouldn't make up for the cost of having a booth, the exposure alone would be a good move for my business. I said okay, I would look into it. So, she left and was talking with other people until Maurette Brown-Clark started singing.

I had begun recording some of the songs she was singing when she sat down at the edge of the stage and started ministering the song *I Have Decided to Follow Jesus*. She said, *"Some of yall are looking around, looking at other business owners, when you know God gave you a vision for your own businesses.....Stop walking around, looking at other people doing what you know you should be doing."* In the video I was recording, you can see Germaine turning around looking for me, and when our eyes met, we both pointed our fingers at each other (God had spoken to me twice within a matter of minutes from two different sources, and I listened). That which was spoken that say was manifested.

Also, just to let you know, Maurette Brown-Clark was backstage during my encounter with Germaine, and she didn't go back there before Maurette came out.

God is in control! My crew, which included myself, Lisa, her daughter Camille, and my two daughters, Jelisa and Tinisha, made up the Daily Desire Team for the Expo in 2018. What a learning experience it was to see all that goes on behind the scenes to get everything and everybody ready. It was awesome to meet, interact with, bond with, and form connections with other vendors.

Getting to hear other people's stories of how they got there, people who come there to vend or even to shop from out of state. The encouragement you receive and pass on to others that should be there and experience it is wonderful to be a part of. I also went back as a vendor again in 2019, and some of the people who visited and talked with us at the table the previous year came back looking for me again, and that's when I started using the term clientele and not customers on a more regular basis.

Germaine, wanting to see me succeed, gave me the opportunity of what it would be like to pitch to Target, even though I wasn't ready, but again the experience of seeing what they were looking for and needed in order to go bigger was a valuable opportunity to have been exposed to. She also highly suggested that I attend the financial session that the bank JP Morgan had set up to talk to business owners about how to get ahead not only with business credit but how to improve their personal credit and financial status. I shared some tips that have actually worked for myself and others where we have seen an increase in our credit score.

Here are a few of those tips:

1. Tally up all your bills and expenses to see what you are truly paying every month.
2. Create a budget.
3. Make the credit card you have that has the highest spending limit, the card you use to pay your reoccurring bills, like gas, electric, cable, phone, and only use it for that purpose.
4. Set up each of your bills to automatically charge that credit card, and keep it locked up and away from your wallet.
5. You must be disciplined in doing this. When you find out what the payment date is of the

credit card, set up your automatic Bill Pay that you were using to pay your bills and set it up instead to pay your credit card balance off, if possible, in two payments before the actual payment date

6. If not, just set up a regular schedule of having a particular amount sent to make payments twice before the due date. The first one should be around three weeks before the due date and the second one around three days before the due date.
7. If your reoccurring bills don't fluctuate too much, you already know how much to have sent per month; just divide the one-month payment into two, and the system will count it as receiving two payments.
8. Watch your credit score change towards the positive and rise.

This is what I like to call a Spring Season mindset.

Thoughts of how I got started writing came to my remembrance as I was working on this book. I was introduced to creative writing in high school and found it interesting. I remember how during that time, I wanted to learn how to play the piano and asked my parents if I could take lessons, so they bought one, and I began lessons with the church musician, Mr. Butler of AME Zion of Newburgh, New York. I realized that I really liked playing the music and rhythms I heard in my mind on TV or on the radio.

For as long as I can remember, I have always had a love for music and playing around on some type of keyboard. There was a picture of me when I was around four or five years old on a 70's type of kid keyboard. My paternal grandmother also had an electronic organ that I used to always play around with, trying to make music.

During the time that I was taking lessons, Mr. Butler had allowed me to play with him a few times in the service, I played on the piano, and I accompanied him on the organ, no particular song, just going with the flow of a melody. Then one day, I wanted to create a song the youth choir I was a part of could sing. I remember writing it, singing and recording the song to a cassette tape, and sharing it with my friend LaWanda from church. I remember her brother Jerome on the drums, and we had a quick session before our choir rehearsal started, where I was playing the music to the song, and he brought in the beats. The song, however, wasn't introduced to the choir, and the tape and words were lost and forgotten about over time, but the memory of me actually doing it remains. So that is my earliest recollection of writing to music.

U***pdates*** from the Fall Season: In 2019, I was given a reminder of the season of the receiving lesson I went through in 2017. I was at the post office to mail off an order to one of my clients, and the window had closed, but the Kiosk was still available. However, I didn't realize that it was also the last day for people to mail off their taxes, so the line was very long to use the kiosk machine. As I got closer, there was an older gentleman ahead of me. He made the statement, *"I don't know how to use this thing, so if yall don't want to be here all night, I will need some help to navigate this thing."* So, people in line laughed, and when I saw no one had stepped out to assist him, I did. All he wanted to do was buy one stamp for a letter he was mailing off. I showed him how to do so; he made his purchase, thanked me for helping, and I said it was my pleasure and then got back in line where the two ladies I stood next to kept my spot for me.

So, as I was listening to what they were talking about, that same older gentleman came up to me and said, *"I want to give you this for taking the time to assist me."* He held out a $10 dollar bill. I said, *"Oh no, sir, that's not necessary. I was glad to help you."* Yall, if you can picture it in your mind, this man's stance and countenance changed, he looked at me with so much sternness, and his voice dropped several octaves and said to me, *"Oh, so you don't know how to receive a blessing do you?"* Instantly, due to my personal relationship, I have taken the time to cultivate and learn how He interacts with me; I shuddered a little bit, looked up and smiled at the Lord, and said Thank You. Then I looked at the gentleman again, opened my hand, and said, *"Yes, I do know how to receive, and I Thank You."* Realize that God will use you, people, you know, just as well as people you don't know to gain your attention when He needs to or test you on lessons He is instilling in you. The people around me that heard the full conversation said, *"Yup, that was God for sure, been there, done that."*

As of 2022, from the start of the position received in 2017, I have continued to grow personally, professionally, financially, and emotionally, having learned new skills and given new opportunities that continue to stretch me out of my comfort zone. Two positions later, I have received an award recognizing my stellar support for the past two years on each contract I was assigned to, which came with a bonus each time, along with a couple of pay raises that allowed me the opportunity to bless others in many different ways, as God allows our paths to intersect. While not forgetting to be a gracious and glad receiver who will ask for assistance when needed and who willingly accepts offers of kindness more quickly when someone wants to bless me!

U*pdates* from the Winter Season: After experiencing the very hellish losses of 2006. In 2007, God turned things around for me. I had grown exponentially spiritually in my walk with God and continued to experience some mighty wonders, like tapping into what He feels when He sees us going through something. I experienced such a deep and profound sadness of weeping when a member of our service baby was stillborn after coming a little bit too early. I wept, not in my normal ways of crying. I experienced such a heaviness, and it felt like anything liquid in my head had poured out into the box of tissue that I went through, wiping my eyes, blowing my nose, and wiping my mouth. I sobbed and wept for an hour straight with that heaviness. When I asked the question about what I had experienced, I was told that sometimes God would allow you to feel a fraction of what He feels. I was glad to have shared that experience, which drew me closer in my walk and relationship with Him.

Also, in 2007, I was tested for my E7 Rank of MSgt and was told during the time that Jelisa was graduating high school, which was significant because my mom and nephews had flown over to the UK to witness her graduation in the knowledge that my Dad and Brother was no longer with us.

Lastly, after applying for a car loan on my own without a co-signer with a credit score of 666 and the loan officer stating that she had to talk with the bank manager. I prayed this simple prayer, *"Lord, if You are going to provide me with the means to pay for this vehicle with all the changes that are about to take place in my life of moving back to the United States with the girls and our dog by myself, then I ask that you allow the transaction to proceed, but if it's not for me in any way shape or form and I won't be able to make the payment to pay it off, please stop this before it gets started. Amen!!!"* The loan officer came back into the room and said, *"We are going to take a chance on you; you have been approved!!!"* All I could do was beam with great joy because God had let me know in that transaction that He was going to take care of me, and He did, and I even paid it off a little early.

By going through all that I have shared in these stories and with the lyrics of each song, you should now see and understand me a little better. You should understand why I am the woman God created me to be and why this once Gospel Album turned book is titled Seasoned by the Seasons of Grace. The following scripture comes to mind that I learned when I was a part of the Sisterhood program we had at the RAF Lakenheath Chapel in the United Kingdom, The Season of Purpose:

Seasoned by the Seasons of Grace

"If you keep quiet at a time like this, deliverance and relief for the Jews will arise from some other place, but you and your relatives will die. Who knows if perhaps you were made queen for just such a time as this?"

Esther 4:14

My response to this is, God Knows!!!

Lord You Are

(Only recorded song actually mastered and available for download on iTunes, Spotify, YouTube, CDBaby)

Lord You are, my everything, the Great I Am, My Savior and King
I trust you Lord, in all You do, in spirit and in truth. I worship You

Guide us Lord and show thy way, In which to go the path You made
We'll follow You and You alone, Our Mighty King Standing at Your throne

The Lord our God Will Reign always, He's worthy of Our worship and praise

Grounded

Intro

Have to stay grounded, through all life's challenges,
trials, and tribulations I need Your help Lord
God gives us the help to stand our ground
Be encouraged my brothers and sisters

Chorus

Don't be afraid
for God is near
He will take care of you
just plant your feet
and stand your ground

Verse One

When you are trying to live your life according to
Christian beliefs
you'll be ostracized (persecuted and endure
suffering), criticized (you're the one with faulty logic)

Cause the foundation on which you stand
Goes against the ways of man
But you have to stay strong in choosing right over wrong

Verse Two

Despite life's problems in which we face, We're guided by the Word of God
It provides us hope that allows us to cope
Don't be ashamed to declare to the world that you're a child of God
Have faith and trust in all that He'll do
He'll never leave nor forsake you

2 Timothy 3:16-17

"All Scripture is inspired by God and profitable for teaching, for reproof, for correction, for training in righteousness; 17 so that the man of God may be adequate, equipped for every good work."

What type of foundation is your life built upon. When building something sustainable, your foundation needs to be strong, sturdy, and immovable. So solid that you are able to withstand the elements that surround you and stay upright. We weren't promised a smooth and easy-going life when we accepted Christ as Lord and Savior. However, when we do go through seasons of storms, turmoil, and strife, we can weather through them. Then God can help us rebuild, repair, and restore our lives from the damages and devastation experienced.

Romans 8:28

"And we know that God causes all things to work together for good to those who love God, to those who are called according to His purpose."

God Is In Control

Intro

In God trust and believe
He'll give you what you need
All you have to know
Is that He is in control

Verse One

Living life each day
by doing things your way
Can't see you've gone astray
Hear what God has to say

Many are the plans
In the mind of a man
But the purpose of the Lord
His Will will always stand

Seasoned by the Seasons of Grace

Chorus

Even with your plans
Things aren't in your hands
Just live within the flow
Because God is in control

In Him trust and believe
He'll give you what you need
All you have to know
Is that God is in control

Verse Two

Problems all around
your mood is always down
You're looking for relief
and it just cannot be found

Don't know which way to turn
Afraid you will get burned
but you can just let go
because God is in control

Ending

CONTROL

Darlene D. Curl

CONTROL
CONTROL
All you have to know
GOD IS IN CONTROL

Intimate Reflections

Closing Song

When We Pray

Chorus

When we Pray

When we Pray

When we Pray

When we Pray

Verse One

First, let us clear our minds

We yield our thoughts to You

We humbly kneel before You

Our souls prostrate before You

Response

When we pray, When we pray

When we pray, When we pray

When we pray, When we pray

When we pray, When we pray

Verse Two

Our hearts, we open them to You

and, Our thirst and hunger is for You

Our spirit longing to join You

Preparing to come before You

Vamp

When We Pray

When We Pray

In Jesus Name

Vamp Two

In Jesus Name

In Jesus Name

In Jesus Name

In Jesus Name

Adlibs

Our Father, which are in heaven, hallowed is thy name, thy kingdom come, thy will be done, on earth

as it is in heaven, give us this day our daily bread and
forgive us our trespasses as we forgive those who
trespass against us, and lead us not into temptation
but deliver us from evil, for thine is the kingdom and
the power and the glory, forever and ever,
Amen.......Amen.........Mmmmmmm........Amen

Additional Writings

The Season of Purpose

Do you know your place in life, are you aware of why
you are here?
You are God's vessel being utilized for His purpose,
which in the beginning may not be so clear.

There will be days when you think and wonder, Lord,
what is happening to me;
Why am I going through this, what is it that I don't
see?

It may be for a short period of time, or it could even
be for years.
And during those moments of wondering, you will
experience both joy and tears.

The Lord will place you in situations and allow you to
experience strife;

But He won't put more on you than you can bear, so
be encouraged as God is in control of your life.

Romans 8:28
For those who love God and are called according to His purpose, ALL things work together for good.
All circumstances in your life are used to chisel you into the image of Christ, who died upon the Cross made out of wood.

First, the Lord will work deep inside your spirit, then proceed out to the surface
Removing all stumbling blocks from your life, including family and friends
That will hinder you because of being no good and worthless.

When God leads you to a place or people where you can be spiritually fed;
Be obedient and stay where He has placed you, so you will grow to endure what lies ahead.

Each issue that you experience may not be just for you alone;

Seasoned by the Seasons of Grace

For our actions and situations can affect others, which can cause either joy or groans.

Why must we go through things, what could be the reason;
They have a direct connection to God's purposes, as Daniel 2:21 says, *He changes the times and the seasons*

Consider this thought when you are going through;
Each situation is its own season of teaching, which God has set up, especially for you

2 Timothy 4:2 reads, *"Preach the word, be ready in season and out of season;*
Reprove, rebuke, and exhort, with complete patience and teaching."
Be prepared for everything and anything at all times
Constantly praying, reading the Word, Praising with hands raised up and reaching

Our ultimate purpose in life is to do God's Will;
And sometimes during our situations, we need to just stop, slow down and be still

Darlene D. Curl

For the Holy Spirit will give directions on just what to say and do,
So, give the Lord your full attention because after that it is all up to you

How do you now view past and present situations, take some time to reflect;
Realize there is a purpose for all of them happening, and remember God is not through with you yet.

Darlene D. Curl

Created Out of the Anointing of God and Recited on March 1, 2008, for the RAF Lakenheath Air Base UK, Gospel Service Women's Sisterhood Bible Study Program

Restored by GOD

To know the purpose of your life, first, you have to understand a few things
Even before the beginning of time as we know it, GOD has been reigning supreme

He is our creator, Alpha - the beginning, and Omega - the end
He sent us His only son JESUS Christ to die, so we can be forgiven of all our sins

The HOLY SPIRIT is a promise and a gift, He was sent to comfort and guide us
He enables our spirit to communicate with GOD, in the precious name of JESUS

All of us who are believers serve a purpose, regardless of who we are and what we do

And from time to time, we must be broken in order
for us to be renewed

For we were created by GOD, in His image, to do and
complete His will
We are to give Him praise and serve Him, but
regardless of us, His plan will still be fulfilled

We were designed to worship Him while living on
this earth
The purpose of our lives already determined, even
before our birth

For we are spirits, within a body of flesh, that has a
soul.
Don't take my word for it, read it for yourself, in the
Bible, that's where it's told

Sometimes our flesh will lead us to believe, we have
arrived, and we have it made,
Especially when we feel as though we have
everything we need, and even those things we crave

Then this causes us to forget about the LORD and/or act like we don't know Him at all
Which is a very sad situation to find ourselves in, just as bad as when man had his first fall

At this point in your spiritual life, you're left feeling shattered and in pieces
Which then ushers in madness and chaos at such a pace that it seems to be never-ending in other words; ceaseless

In that very moment of our lives, we find ourselves broken,
Not understanding how we got here and not having any words left to be spoken

But don't be in despair or worry, for GOD knows just what to do
For He will use that very brokenness in the rebuilding and renewal of you

You must focus your attention on Jesus when you become tired, confused, and lost

Because the problem and situation you may be going through could very well be your assigned cross

So, what you need to understand and have the ability to see,
This is what the LORD said in Matthew 16:24, *"Let man deny himself and take up his cross and follow Me."*

Do your part, trust, and have faith, just like the Bible said
In James, second chapter verse 26, *"faith without works is dead."*

So, believe when the LORD finishes His work, within His own time, that you will be restored
But not to how you previously were, you'll be greater than you were before

For GOD's restoration is about bringing joy to your spirit and having you closer to Him
Returning you to the path, He originally set for you, guiding you from a life of sin

Seasoned by the Seasons of Grace

Always remember, we must give glory, honor, and praise to whom it is do
Because GOD, JESUS, and the HOLY SPIRIT, is the restoration already residing within you.

Created Out of the Anointing of God and Recited on June 9, 2007, for Women's Program Being Hosted by New Life

Darlene D. Curl

Darlene D. Curl

Tears of joy come to my eyes
When I can see the morning skies
For I know that God has made a way
For me to see another day

But if one day I don't awake
Please don't make the serious mistake
Of thinking that I have gone away
For in your heart, I will always stay.

I'll be watching you from up in Heaven
Where I will be with all my brethren
So don't be sad or cry or moan
Because I'll be with God at my new home.

Created in High School in an insert for my Yearbook
called the 1988 Colonnade
Darlene Robinson

Seasoned by the Seasons of Grace

The following are some poems created, written, and recited during my first deployment (from January to May 2005) during the weekly poetry nights.

A Daughter's Love

(Written and recited March 24, 2005)

Sugar and spice and everything nice, that's what little girls are made of
That was the rhyme I heard at a time when I was just a little young thing

Now I'm grown with two girls of my own, I wonder if they think as I do

Nothing is more precious except God Above when it comes to the genuine feelings of a Daugther's Love

I've always been known as a daddy's girl, the twinkle in his eye, the one who changed his world
For I'm the one they said would never be, the doctors claimed he had no seed

But here I am, I proved them wrong, for a Daughter's
Love is very strong

Mama taught me lessons, she started when I was
young
I didn't understand her reasons, I just like to have fun

But now I appreciate just what she did for me
My love for her has grown and grown, As I expand
the family tree
With both parents getting older, sickness threatens
their health
For the longevity of their lives, I'd trade away all
amounts of wealth

These past few months have left me hurt
Their little girl Dee who they used to call squirt

But I am strong, through God Above
Who is also my Father and who has His Daughter's
Love

Candles Upon My Cake

(Written April 25, 2005, and recited April 28, 2005)

Well, this week I celebrate 35 candles upon my cake
What does it mean? It says a lot, it's time to reflect on all I got

I'm a daughter to both parents, who are still married and alive
Sister to a brother, five years younger than I

A wife of 15yrs going on 16 in November, my husband is also a tech Sgt and Air Force Member
I'm a mother of 2 daughters, 15 & 10, I even have a dog who depends on me like a friend.

I have been many places and have seen a lot, come across some very good people and some who are not

Seasoned by the Seasons of Grace

Every day of my life I know I'm Blessed, for that, I
thank God for whatever comes next,
Age ain't nothing but a number, just like Aaliyah
said, it's all about how you feel inside your heart,
soul, and head

As far as I'm concerned life really is great, As I count
each one of my 35 candles upon my cake

My Gift to you

(Written and recited March 31, 2005)

Sit back, relax and close your eyes
I'm about to give you a big surprise
Take a deep breath and hold it for a while
Now let it out in a slow and careful style
That right there is how you start
The cleansing of your stressful heart
A few precious seconds of this may not seem long
But your body will say thank you as it lives on
So, every now and then this is what you should do
For the instant release of stress is my gift to you

A New perspective

(Written and recited April 7, 2005)

Imagine an empty jar that represents your birth
Add a few rocks to it to show your years on earth
Take a look at the jar, does it seem like there's a lot
Can you fill it up with many more, for the years you think you got

Well, let's flip the script and do this in reverse
Put in as many rocks, according to statistics, first
Then year after year, you take one out
For however old you are, make sure you have the right count

Now, look at your jar, does it still seem full
Do you still have plenty of years yet ahead of you?

This different perspective of thinking should have you reexamine your life

Are you living it to the fullest, are you doing it right?

Are you letting those who you care about know just
how you feel?

Or do you maintain it within yourself because you're
keeping it real?

Well, life is too short and can be taken away without a
moment's notice

So, look at your life with a new perspective and
readjust to show this

Rhythm of Life

(Written and recited April 14, 2005)

If the sun is shining brightly and everything is going your way
You don't have anything to complain about, you're having a very good day

But then at a moment's notice, it all turns really bad
Everything seems to be going wrong and it leaves you fiery mad

When a situation like that happens, it will cause you a lot of strife
One minute you're up and then you're down such is the *Rhythm of Life*

One day you're sittin at home, chillin with your fam
Kids are playing with the dog while you have a drink with your man

Then you are told
You are going to deploy
You get about a week to get ready
Now you're getting annoyed

Then a loved one gets sick, it all happens at the same time
You ask the Lord for strength before you lose your mind

In a very quick tempo, circumstances increase
It beats and beats you down real low, there seems to be no relief

You give your all at a job you have never done before
The phones keep ringing off the hook
You want to slam them on the floor
But then someone says to you, thank you for all you do
I appreciate you helping me with sincerity that is true
So, when you feel yourself shifting going from left to right
Just remember to go with the flow, for this is the *Rhythm of Life*

My Rainbow

(Written and recited May 5, 2005)

From light as white to dark as the night
All the colors of my rainbow are beautiful to the sight

All different shades, tones, and hues
Redbone, high yellow, sexy chocolate, and midnight
Blue

Crème Brulé, caramel, butter pecan and honey
butterscotch, peanut butter boy, don't we sound
yummy
Coffee, hot chocolate, cognac and brandy,
cappuccino, mocha, we are hot, have spirit and sweet
like candy

All these names describe a warm and colorful people
we come from different backgrounds but yet we are
all equal

Because regardless of the package we may come in
What counts is the substance of our being and not the coloring of our skin

Even though the colors I described earlier are what is most familiar to me
My Family and friends and people who I keep close
Are made up of different races and nationalities

White, Black, Italian, Japanese, German, African
Hispanic, Portuguese, Jamaican, Korean, combinations of different nations

My heart is always open to all of God's creation, I do love my rainbow and how diverse it is, and this will be yet another thing that I will pass down to my kids.

God's Time

(Written and recited April 28, 2005)

When you hear this term, what comes to your mind
For me it's the old folks who say, Baby Everything happens in *God's Time*

My personal revelation of this fact lets me know how people are seasoned it goes hand in hand with God's Plan
And everything happens for a Reason

I now can see why through my years; I have been placed in situations that have caused me countless tears
All the headaches and pains I have gone through, wondering why this is happening to me, what did I do?

Darlene D. Curl

The challenges I face while at work being assigned
tasks that causes my head to hurt
The type of personalities I didn't like to be around
became a part of my every day for several years now

The tasks assigned when I wasn't ready, now I'm in
charge of those things to make everything go smooth
and steady each trial and tribulation were steps to
prepare me

For I would meet up with those troubles again and
again but each time magnified ridiculously

It's funny when you can reflect in hindsight and say
yeah God has a sense of humor

He builds us up through each of our encounters,
storms of problems, and endless rumors

One day we will receive all that we need, even when
we complain and whine because everything that is
meant to be will happen but only in *God's Time.*

Catch 22

(Written and recited May 5, 2005)

What can you do, where can you go?
Each turn you take comes to a dead-end role

You find yourself trapped between a hard place and a wall
There's no way out, there's no room to crawl

You're damned if you do, you're damned if you don't
It has a hold of you and let go it won't

It ties your hands and binds your feet, it makes you sour when once you were sweet
Catch 22 I'm talking about you, you leave us no choices; you quiet our voices; nothing can be said, it's like we are dead *Catch* 22 I'm talking about you

But then again, there's one way out, all you have to
do is fall on your knees and begin to shout
My Heavenly Father help me please for You are the
only One who can bring me at ease

You can reach down and lift me up, open all the
doors that once were struck
Bring back our voice, in which we can sing a
counteraction to what a *Catch* 22 brings

You make options available both left and right we
come alive again with a new sight so be aware I'm not
affected by you *Catch* 22 you are now through

A Woman's Worth

(Written and recited May 12, 2005)

Who are you and what do you represent, do people
see the real you in your truest essence?
Are you free to be yourself and not someone's
puppet? Are you always put together or do you like
to rough it?

Are you only known as someone's mother, wife, or
friend? Are you always the caregiver and provider to
no end?

Do you have your own identity outside of those
things, do you know who you are and are you in
touch with your personal being?
Women you are much more special than what you
realize but yet you let just anyone in between your
thighs

You're often taken advantage of and don't even know
it, but sooner or later it will catch up to you when you
have forgotten that you even sowed it

Worthy worthy is what you are you sparkle like a
diamond and shine like a bright star

Embrace the beauty you have within and treat
yourself as your best friend

For it is with you where the need is and starts first,
how can you give of yourself when you still hunger
and thirst

Whether you consider yourself to be a girl, woman, or
lady, self-respect starts within and not by being dirty
and shady

There is a great joy to be found in being of sound
mind and alive, especially a woman who finally
comes to realize

Her role, need and purpose on earth are made crystal
clear when she finds her own worth

Sensuality

(Written and recited May 19, 2005)

Like fine wine aged by time, so soft sweet, and
smooth
Exotic erotic like the slow jams of old
That quickly gets you in the mood

Sexy and attractive, making heads turn, both male
and female passions begin to burn

Sophistication is shown at its best in the way you
walk, talk and even in the way you dress

It is more than the physical it will make you feel full
the topic of this particular poem is not sex but being
sensual

Darlene D. Curl

Sex is way too easy there's no challenge in it just
show some skin and bam you are in it and it only
takes a minute

But sensuality is totally different and involves so
much more it's like the feeling you get while
watching the sunset off a far and distant shore

It's embedded within your whole self and is reflected
in all that you do, the way you think and carry
yourself, and how you interact with others too.

Pure joy will come to your soul, and you will glow
like the sun at noon, when sensuality is a part of you
you'll radiate like flowers when in full bloom

The Final Finger Snap

(Written and recited May 19, 2005)

Four months ago, I was told I had to leave the comfort
of my home, report to a base in a desert place where
everything looks dried to the bone
Then one day while walking around, my friend and I
came to the lyrical lounge, a place for people to lay
their talents down. Founded by a soulful and
talented woman by the name of Dawn Brown

Just like in Love Jones poetry was in need and tonight
my final poem will be about the Deid.

This right here was my first deployment compared to
where I could have gone this has been a real
enjoyment

Eat 24/7 at the dining facility or go to Pizza Hut,
Subway or Burger King, have dessert at Baskin

Robbins, or go by the pool and have yourself some Dairy Queen
There's one thing I won't miss and leaves me wondering why what is the purpose and the function of the darn aggressive flies

There were a lot of things that took place and events you could attend, I'm going to give you what I can remember, so temporarily my rhyming will end

Chapel, Jacks, and Andy's, two or three comedy shows, Bands, talent show, sports day, fire muster, casino night, marathons, Base BBQs, squadron BBQs, Mardi Gras parade, movies at the theater and community center, pool, karaoke, bingo, break dancing, salsa, intramural sports basketball, volleyball, dodgeball, and a couple of pool parties

So as you can see there were a lot of events while some people chose to just chill and listen to the music under the big tent

Seasoned by the Seasons of Grace

I myself worked hard, did some studying and drank
beer, met a lot of different people, and learned a few
things about how some act while they are here

I found a new avenue of expression that I didn't
realize was within, I will continue to write from time
to time
Poetry, which has become a new friend.

So, when the last words are spoken and my poem
comes to a wrap instead of you clapping let me hear
your fingers snap.

The following are other writings, songs or poems started but not completed....

Praise Through the Storm

No matter what may come my way
For You, I will always give You the Highest Praise
Through every tear that may form
I vow to Praise You through the Storm

When I stumble in life's winds and rains
Through all the mishaps that bring a lot of pain
Nothing will ever separate my love for You
Your sacrifice taught me that You're faithful and true.

Darlene D. Curl

He Won't Leave

You say there's nothing new under the sun
Not what I say or the things I've done
But still, I try to run and hide
Like You weren't there during those times

How can it be that You won't leave?
When I do wrong and go along
With what I see and what I hear
I need You, Lord, I need You near

God Your Word states several times
That You will never leave us nor forsake us
However, there are times when our flesh gets so weak
That we start to question if You are still with us
Like Jesus Christ on the night of Him being crucified
hanging on the Cross
He cried out My God My God why have You
forsaken me

But the reality is You are ever-present with us and it
is our circumstances that have us feeling distant from
You
Which is why we feel the need to say, Lord please
don't leave me

Darlene D. Curl

The Love of Christ

The Love of Christ is better than life
The Love of Christ it feels so right
The Love of Christ He gave His life
The Love of Christ
The Love of Christ

I never knew what true love was
Until I witnessed the Love of Jesus
I Love Him because He first loved me
Unconditionally, He gave His Life on a tree
This agape Love has truly changed my Life
Freed from Sin because Jesus Christ Paid the Ultimate Price

Christ Love is the Best Love
There is no Higher Love, No Greater Love, Unfailing Love, Fulfilling Love, Forgiving Love, Unconditional Love

Seasoned by the Seasons of Grace

There's nothing like it, open your heart to receive
Christ
Embrace it and experience new life
Share it with those young and old
Treasure it like its precious gold

Living Christian

I Love Jesus, I can't help it
I'm *Living Christian* and don't regret it
He saved my soul now I'm indebted
Yes, I love Jesus, I can't help it
Yes, I am bold when I proclaim
My love for Jesus and I'm unashamed
For He is worthy of all my Praise
And I will do it for the rest of my days

I will testify of all His goodness
Who He is and What He has done for me
I accept His guidance and His discipline
Want you to know I really love me some Him

I'm Still Standing

I'm still standing
I'm still standing
I'm still standing
I'm still standing

After the storm clouds have blown away
The sun will come out to a brand-new day
Sorrows will be left back in yesterday
The joy of the morning has made its way

Its morning and I made it through the night
I might have some scars from the battle of the fight
But overall, the victory has been won
Because of my Father and His son

I got knocked down, but not knocked out
I stand to my feet so that I can shout
I'm alive and well to see another day

Darlene D. Curl

That's how I know things will be okay

Heart and Soul

I give my *Heart and Soul* to Jesus
Lord, I give my *Heart and Soul* to You
I give my *Heart and Soul* to Jesus
Lord, I give it all to You

I sacrifice my heart, my mind, and my soul
Lord, I give to You all that I am

The ultimate price is what You paid
To wipe my slate clean for judgment day
Your Amazing Grace is what set me free
Your Love for me was given unconditionally

Get Away

Fly away, I want to *Get Away*
No time to waste, I need some space
Helicopter, Jet, or plane
Destination sun with no chance of rain

So much is going on, I don't even know where to start
I'm feeling very overwhelmed like I'm falling apart
So many demands are being placed on my time
I'm being pulled in too many directions all at the same time

I feel like if one more thing is added I might just snap
Just like a wild caged animal who feels cornered and trapped
Needing to be like Jesus when asleep on the boat, that's until
He rebuked the winds and waves, saying Be Quiet and Still

Seasoned by the Seasons of Grace

I'm not packing a bag just leaving everything behind
So, I can get to a place where I can relax and unwind
I'm not telling a soul just getting up and go
To a location that is secluded, just God and I and no one else included

Darlene D. Curl

Quiet Place

Here in this *Quiet Place*
where You have brought me
Far from the noises
with the Word, You've taught me

In this Holy Temple
I will give You praises
Humbled at the knowledge
of Your sovereign greatness

Take me away

Take me away
to the *Quiet Place*

Broken Hearts

I need Your Love Lord God
I need Your Love Lord
I need Your Love
I need Your Love
Send It

Beat down, defeated, no hope, and depleted
Hated, mistreated vicious cycles of this repeated

This world is so cold, people wanting to be consoled
Lord, it has to come from You, a love like the morning dew

About the Author

Darlene was born on April 25th, 1970, in Newburgh, New York, to the Late Henry Robinson and her mother, Veronica Robinson, as well as being the big sister to the Late Dexter Robinson. She is a divorced mother of two adult daughters, Jelisa and Tinisha, and has a 6-year-old granddaughter named Justus, who will turn seven this year, who affectionately refers to her as VoVo (Grandmother in Portuguese) and has another granddaughter on the way, arriving in October of 2022.

After Graduating from Newburgh Free Academy aka "NFA" High school, class of 1988, she then enlisted into the United States Air Force in October of that same year and retired on November 1, 2012, as a Master Sergeant (E7), after serving 24 years in various Administrative, Computer Assistance, and Knowledge Operations Management positions. Her military career took her around the world to eight duty station assignments; Texas, Germany twice, Pentagon, Korea, Japan, England, Maryland, and Deployed three times to Southwest Asia.

Darlene has a Bachelor of Arts Degree in Psychology from the American Military University. Some of her interests are attending events with family and friends at wine festivals, dining at restaurants, listening to live music, dancing, BBQing, and taking pictures (she is referred to by friends as the historian). She loves working in her garden, cooking, baking, and grilling (she has a family event every other month named Iron Chef Our Way with postings on Facebook and Instagram).

She is an adventurous soul that likes to travel and is in her element during nature walks and hiking. Darlene is also a bit of an adrenalin junkie, having accomplished a Tandem Skydive, riding roller coasters, zip-lining, and jumping off some waterfalls in the Dominican Republic.

In 2016 after being divinely inspired by God, Darlene created Daily Desire LLC (www.dailydesire425.com), making and selling online and at vendor events Homemade Skincare Products. She originally created the moisturizing skin cream for friends as a homemade Christmas Gift a couple of years prior. After several other people showed an interest in purchasing the product, along with receiving positive feedback about the quality & results of using samples of it, the business was born by the state of Maryland, on April 25th, 2016.

Darlene currently resides in Waldorf, Maryland.

About the Publisher

The Vision to Fruition Publishing House offers a variety of publishing options.

The Vision to Fruition Publishing House has earned its positive reputation because we go out of our way to provide truly exceptional service to each of our customers, something we like to call - "The White Glove Experience."

We believe that publishing a book is about more than becoming an author. It's about bringing a vision to fruition, building an audience, and expanding your influence.

Not all publishers are created equal, and we know that when extra attention is required, our "White Glove Experience" will not disappoint.

As an experienced team of authors as well, we specialize in coaching you through the publishing process and bringing your vision to fruition.

www.ingramcontent.com/pod-product-compliance
Lightning Source LLC
Chambersburg PA
CBHW021231090426
42740CB00006B/484

9781735835969